LOSING
LIGHT

A Journey Through Grief

Suzanne Laurent

To Dave

Peace & Light

Suzanne ♡

Copyright © *Losing Light* by Suzanne Laurent

Cover photo by Suzanne Laurent
Photos by Suzanne Laurent
Author photo by Ioanna Raptis

Published by Piscataqua Press
an imprint of RiverRun Bookstore
142 Fleet Street
Portsmouth, NH 03801

ISBN: 978-1-944393-60-1

For my son Luc, who brings back the light.

Contents

Preface

I. Losing Light

II. Steel Gray Sorrow

PHOTOS

Cover
"Umbrellas over Avignon"

Preface

When my husband died suddenly following an unfortunate series of medical events, I turned to a comforting source of solace familiar to me – writing poetry.

At first I kept the poems to myself, but started putting one out there once in a while on social media. The reactions of friends comforted me and encouraged me to share the collection of poems I wrote during the two years since losing my other half after almost 30 years of marriage on Feb. 22, 2015.

These are two quotes from friends that especially inspired me:

"One of the many amazing things about you, Suzanne – you use the pain inside of you like it's paint, squeezing it out of the tube onto the canvas of your page to paint these powerful poems that share your journey so fully and honestly.

"I'm blown away every time by your words and the images they paint for me of what you must be going through. I'm moved, and saddened, and heartened all at the same time because of what you've had, and what you've lost, and how strong you are to put it all out there and keep putting one foot in front of the other." ~ Ola Lessard

"Let your heart explode – as if it had a choice – and all the tiny pieces will fall at our feet. One by one we will collect them, and carry them back to you – honoring all that you are, all that you have been through, and all that you have lost. You will be our teacher, and we will bring you home." ~ Pamela Wallace

Kate Leigh, Portsmouth (NH) Poet Laureate (2015-2017), also told me poems were meant to be shared, especially poems about grief, as they may help in the healing process for someone else.

Interspersed with the poems about my husband, Jean Bernard, are other losses – of a baby, a friend and parents. Grief does not go away, I've found, but it alters you and becomes part of who you are, and you learn somehow to accept it.

I. Losing Light

"Infinity"

Premonition

Sauntering down Ceres Street
in the indigo December twilight,
mist envelops the tugboats
                along the river.
Silence as thick as the fog,
                not a soul around.

Windows reflect the season,
flower boxes overflow
        with holly, pine cones, juniper.
Pausing in front of
                an old wooden door,
something tugs at me.
A feeling I can't shake.
My heart hears a ghostly whisper –
                I will soon be alone.

The Tide

The breeze pulled me out of myself,
ocean calling me at sunset to
                    inhale the day's end,
and exhale the memories
in my head, in my heart
that are relentless,
                    some days suffocating.
The salty mist against orange light
washed over me as the tide pulled
into a deep space of regret,
                    a longing for all that is lost.

Maple Manhattan

Five o'clock,
aged wooden bar
reminiscent of
a timeless space
          in Paris.

Flurries of snow dust
the glass panes of windows,
          an early March surprise.
Trees tapped for sap,
soon to be boiled down
          to sweetness.

A smoky drink of bourbon,
bitters, splash of maple syrup,
          echoes of a bittersweet winter.

A small booze-soaked cherry
lingers on the tongue
like so many
kisses once savored
          during riper seasons.

March Morning

Snow dusts the forest
like confectioner's sugar,
concealing the hint
    of the coming mud season.

Soft amber light
eerily peeks through
from the wetlands beyond
with the promise
       of an extra hour
of sunlight next week.

Maple trees drip sap
like tears
that well up from
    the thawing heart of winter.

March Is A Fickle Month

March is a fickle month.
Sap drips from maple trees
while winds sting and
tears fall from unprotected eyes.

A warm day
suddenly turns bitterly cold,
much like the twists
in relationships
that drink in the sweet syrup of words,
but often trip in the thawing ground,
muddied by memories of
a past never brought to light.

Yellow April

April is a bittersweet month,
filled with the yellow sweetness
of daffodils and garlands of forsythia.
You planted these along a stone wall,
the first to bloom on our land.

My best friend, just a teenager,
died at the beginning of April.
My mother left so many years later,
on the last day of the month,
made as bitter as the cancer that claimed them.

The promise of warmer weather
can suddenly turn into a few inches of snow.
Yet buds appear on star magnolias,
and hope blooms in a heart
long jaded by life's twisted turns.

"Star Magnolias"

Star Magnolias

The sweet scent
of star magnolias
wafting from
the park nearby
the place we last lived
takes my breath away.

Paths around the monument,
dedicated to the brave,
are scattered with white petals.

The air was warm today,
reminiscent of happier times
when we would
turn our faces to the sun
and welcome the season
as our dog rolled in grass,
freed of the snow of winter.

I sit in solitude as memories
float off with wispy white clouds
in a cobalt blue sky.

Black Saturday

The day before Easter,
a time for reflection
after the day Jesus was put to death
when those he trusted betrayed him.

The ground is still bare of springtime,
mud encircles autumn's leftover yellow grass.
Parents brighten the barren fields
with neon-colored plastic eggs
filled with candies, coins and small treats.

We await the arrival of sunnier days,
times filled with laughter,
the saltwater sting of tears
receding from the bleakness of winter.
Pussy willows and lilies bring that promise
                    of new life without you.

Spinning

Saturdays suck now.
Home was always my refuge
after a day of covering news.
Climbing the stairs,
inhaling the scent of the onion soup
                              you often made,
a warm welcome.

Sundays are shot now, too.
Reading the paper in bed
with coffee and fruit,
                              cats content.
It was a day to explore the coast,
stopping for a random repast.

Couples reflect in restaurant windows,
couples laughing,
holding hands on the sidewalk.

We orbited around each other's lives.
                              Now, I spin alone.

"Daylilies"

Strength to Survive

How do I respond to the
well-meant observation,
      'You're so strong,'
when I feel as fragile
as an ice-covered branch
a strong wind would send
shattering into shards
      onto the pavement?

From dawn to sunset
a daylily blooms just once;
its survival brief
      in the patterns of life.
A dozen more disguise
its demise with the next sunrise.
Strength comes with the
fresh bloom of the new day,
      weakens as the light fades.

Darkness

They were the sparks of light
we shared together.
Fireflies on a sultry June night
dancing through the forest,
goldfinches showing off their summer plumage,
a quarter moon with Venus
              dripping off the bottom,
lightning and shooting stars,
copper penny oak leaves
              against an autumn sky,
diamonds glistening on fresh snowfall.

You dimmed the lights
              as you left.

Autumn's Closing In

Nights are getting cooler.
Autumn's closing in,
bringing memories
of apple pies,
carved pumpkins,
walking through
           the woods
over trails you made,
leaves crunching underfoot.
Our gentle dog has joined you
in eternal slumber.
The garden swing is still now,
the golden paths untrodden.

"End of Autumn"

Losing Light

Bright orange gourds
grin and grimace on All Hallows Eve.
Candles flicker and embers linger
       in bonfires, pits and fireplaces.
Smoke of spirits
floats out of chimneys
towards the heavens
if you believe that
your lost loved ones
       are on the nightside of the stars.
The eleventh month arrives,
recognizing the dead on its second day.
Evenings soon lose light,
as we draw inward,
a time of reflection,
       of embracing fleeting memories.

Advent Anticipation

Advent calendars
always brought anticipation –
cookies baking,
a crèche built on the mantle,
'The Messiah', *'The Nutcracker'*,
'A Christmas Story'.
A tree of cherished ornaments,
some handmade since kindergarten.

The little doors opened
each day with that small tinge of hope.

The first of December.
bare trees, dark afternoons,
no open doors this year
            of closing too many.

Out of Rhythm

The rhythm of the holiday season
                    is gone.
A house full of people,
roaring fire, Kirs to toast
and turkey roasting.
One by one, people left,
for another place,
here or beyond.

I live in another space now.
Memories packed in boxes
that will stay there for now.
My heart would bleed to look at even
                    one ornament.

"Flickering Light"

Quarter Moon Flight

Quarter moon outside
my tiny window seat
guides the plane
on its westbound journey
across the country.
Ocean to ocean
ending a year of loss,
                of change,
of a heart patched by the kindness
of unexpected encounters.

There is always that feeling
of being in a safe time
and space.
It can go in the blink
                of an eye.

But the sun still shines,
rainbows appear after storms,
and during a pause
on a misty morning,
you feel enveloped
in all that is good.
And you get a sense
that maybe everything
might be all right –
                if just for now.

Christmas Eve

Christmas Eve,
always so magical,
anticipating a snow-covered yard
in the early morning.
Birds feeding on seeds,
us sipping coffee,
a fire lit,
torn wrapping paper,
while a small child
looked to see if Santa ate the cookies
before opening presents.
Sweet memories
like so many clicks
of film frames,
stored forever in archival boxes
that can't be opened in
the harsh reality of daylight.

Reverse Flight

Remnants of the first
snowfall of the season
await as the nonstop flight
crosses the country in the glare of
the sun outside my tiny window seat.

It's been a nonstop year of sorrow and loss.
A Christmas trip to change up things
worked somehow,
but memories can't be
erased from a heart
full of life's shrapnel.

New memories made,
some smiles, some laughs,
tucked into a suitcase.
They will have to somehow find their
place in a corner of my new life.

II. Steel Gray Sorrow

"Gray Light"

Steel Gray Sorrow

A sliver of steel gray sky,
bruised by yellow sunset light,
catches my breath.
January black ice cautions
the steps I take,
during the bleakest month,
knowing that is how
I lost you one year ago.

I gather opaque sea glass tears
from beaches we have walked,
as grief chisels
at unasked questions.
Pieces of puzzles that never
quite fit after many years together –
                you took them all with you.

Last Week, Last Year

Last week, last year
was a blur of finalizing details
for your funeral,
family gathering from across
            corners of the country.

Choosing photos, music, words –
wrapping three decades
            into a snapshot
for those who came to say goodbye.

A year later,
it is still a blur of confusion.
Insurance forms, taxes, checkbooks,
            the tidy things of life,
all changed to a single name.
One by one, a signature erases the life
            we shared together.

First Year Without My Valentine

The early years
brought romance and anticipation,
sweet sentiments and candlelight
on the day devoted to love.

Dinners for two,
gave way to more practical
dinners at home,
fireplace lit,
still fanning flames.

Years later, dinners out again,
champagne toasts
to love that had languished
over the familiarity
of years.

Last year, an early morning
surprise visit to the rehab center,
flowers to brighten a dreary room,
our dog delighted by
the brief reunion.

No sweet words, champagne,
no hearts or kisses,
just a longing ache,
this first year without you.

Last Days

Fourteen years ago
sometime during the night,
my father took his last breath
ending years of World War II shrapnel
that never freed his mind,
his heart,
his body,
ravaged by diabetes,
years of neglect finally taking its toll
on the man who was a shadow
                                    all my life.

One year ago,
my husband left
the place we last lived by ambulance,
he, too, a shadow
of the man I met who had
so much curiosity and interest,
and memories of growing up
in post-war Paris,
as the boots of Hitler's army
marched out of
                        the City of Light.

"Cold Light"

Adrift

Startled awake
earlier than usual that morning,
a blurry drive to the hospital.
You were already gone,
                moments before I arrived.

For three hours
I sat frozen by your side, still warm,
before staggering back out into
                the bleak February morning.

Family scattered in time zones
kept me from sharing the sad news
I had to process alone for a while,
                adrift on a floe of sorrow.

A year has passed,
a circle imprinted on my finger
like a tattoo where I wore your ring,
from that promise of
'Until death do us part',
                so long ago.

Rain on Snow

You came to this country
            from France
so many years ago
on a Valentine's Day,
        long before we met.

Years later,
we shared a sweetheart's dinner,
knowing I was carrying
our second child
        who left us at birth.

Your father died
that February night.
A trip to France
to bring him back to Paris,
to rest with your mother.

Last February
the snow was relentless
as I tried to visit you after the fall
that broke your arm,
and ultimately tore my heart
                into pieces.
Today's rain melts the snow
like so many warm tears falling
on memories,
        forever frozen in time.

Daylight Savings Time

Extra hour of light
that saved me
from sinking into darkness
last year,
less than a month
       after you left.

It is different
this year.
I embrace the light,
but often fall into the
dark memories
of things never resolved,
       unfinished endings.

Equinoxes

The artist in you
would see Impressionism
each spring
when the delicate bloom of branches
traced the brick buildings
in the city where we met.

In autumn, you saw the same
muted patterns
among the birch trees in the cemetery
where our baby's body
was laid to rest,
but not her spirit.
A tiny white feather
floating along a creek in Sedona,
showed me that.

You now lie across from her
facing the birches.
But your spirit
soars every time I see
a seagull just out of the corner
of my line of vision.

Drowning Rain

The rain pours down
relentlessly tapping on my roof,
my windows,
my heart.
Tears flow freely.
There is water everywhere,
I feel like I'm drowning
in random memories that creep up
unexpectedly,
like those moments
when you awaken startled
from a bad dream,
only to realize it's all too real.
Years under restless blankets –
gone.
That feeling of being held,
safe from the storm,
still pulls
on this warm April night.

Another Surreal Season

I took a detour from the day,
walking the beach at sunset.
People partying,
opening their
second homes for summer.
Kids, dogs, picnics,
reminiscent of days
I once thought would never end.

Alone, I navigated
seaweed, seashells and tiny rocks.
The wind was a gentle caress
coming off pewter waves
lapping at my toes,
while the salty air
sometimes mingled with
a tear or two.

Strawberry Solstice

Born on the first day of summer,
the strawberry moon this year
brought your spirit
      back through the sphere of timelessness,
remembering those first ripened berries
          warm on our lips.
You, now on the other side of all we once knew,
the sweetness of the season leaves a bitter taste
         on the longest day of the year.

Full Moon Baby

You'll always be my baby girl.
For forty-one minutes you tried,
but here just wasn't where you
wanted to stay.

It's not easy to be human.
Better to return to a safer place
amongst innocent angels.

The moon was full that night
as it is now.
Twenty-two years have passed,
but my body
still holds the memory
of the time we had together –
                    our only time.

October

Leaves float down,
pirouetting from branches,
covering the forest in gold.

So many autumns,
so many memories
of leaves crunching underfoot,
of days devouring the palette
of copper penny oak leaves,
russet maples, orange gourds.

Of seeing the setting moon as the sun rose
on shorter days.

"Winter Lights"

Broken Village

I never wanted a collection.
Maybe photos that could tell stories,
but not coins, stamps,
        or other such meaningless things.
My mother gave me a Dickens Village gristmill,
        all those years ago,
a memory of our marriage
                        at the Wayside Inn.
The village grew into a newspaper stand,
a coffee shop, a book store, a skating rink,
                        reminiscent of times, jobs, fun –
slices of life over so many years.
It was the first of the season's decorations
                        painstakingly set up
after Thanksgiving each year.
The tiny lights of the village
                        are turned off this season.

III. Chasing Shadows

"Seine Sunset"

Towards Your Home

Over the Atlantic,
crossing the space between
                our two worlds.

Three decades have traveled
since the first time we held hands
                as the flight took off
bringing me to your homeland.

You showed me
your favorite places,
the shadowed spaces
near the Louvre,
the cold grassless cemetery
where I met your mother –
                a name on a stone.

I do not find you in Paris.
The cacophony
of the city shorts out the
memories we had so long ago,
when the magic
                was still electric.

Speeding South

Tiny contained villages
appear, disappear
in the blink of an eye,
as the train
hurtles towards the
south of the country
            of your birth.

Sunflower fields have
lost their bloom,
fields dried up of their harvest.

My heart is turned inside out
searching for memories of
happier times.

Tears blur the countryside,
competing with speed,
for glimpses of the past
            that won't appear.

"Full Moon over Agde"

Last Night in Agde

The full moon traces the rooftops
of a town once vibrant,
                              now asleep.

Rue de l'Amour,
such a suggestive name,
scents of lavender,
aperitifs on terraces,
holding hands along alleyways.

The little village is slowly dying
as modern convenience has found
its way to even this ancient town.
Shuttered storefronts,
faded memories cached inside,
                              forever.

Umbrellas over Avignon

A rainbow of open umbrellas
hangs over a marble walkway.
They cannot shield
the Mistral tempest
that tears through the ancient city,
the relentless wind,
that stirs memories of warmer days,
when all I had to discover
                              was you.

Gare de Lyon

The train speeds back to Paris
from places that once felt like home.

I am a stranger now
                    without you there.

Our son has fleeting glimpses
                    of childhood trips.
We shared what we could pull from the
crumbling ancient walls,
                    making new memories.

We first met so many years ago this day at sunset.
Why can't I find you anywhere?

This sojourn has
made me homesick
for my new solitary chapter in a
healing seaport on the
                    other side of the Atlantic.

"Shuttered"

Chasing Shadows

A tear escapes,
trickles down my cheek
as the plane makes its ascent
leaving behind
      the City of Lights.

For two weeks I
chased shadows down
cobblestoned alleyways.
      I could not catch
           a glimpse of you.

I came to this place
to heal the elusive pain
           that never quite
surfaced since you left.

I carry it back home.

IV. Backside of the Night Stars

"Daybreak"

Widow's Walk

The tide was out,
leaving an expanse
        of ripples on the sand.
It was the sweet spot
of the evening light that turns
                the landscape pinkish-orange.

Abandoned sand castles crumbling,
words etched by twigs
succumbing to waves
                depositing seaweed, sea glass.
My solitary shadow,
stretched by the sun's low position.

A lone seagull circles again and again.
You always said you'd like to be a bird.

Memory Boxes

Beatle cards,
letters to a friend met on vacation,
prom tickets,
friendship ring,
Polaroid photos.
Teenage trinkets
fill a memory box.

Box of cards when my mother
died,
to say 'I'm sorry'.
Boxes of photographs,
black and white memories
from years long ago.

A little trunk holds
tiny inked hand and footprints
a lock of hair, a flowered dress, a doll,
a box of a future that never came
when our baby died.

Another box sits on a table
next to an empty chair.
More cards,
more words of sympathy.
My other half is gone.

I need a box of innocent sunshine again.

Apple Trees in Winter

Gnarled black trunks lined in rows
across the frozen ground,
limbs freed of their autumn weight,
branches making patterns
          on newly fallen snow,
last leaves still clinging
          like so many dried up tears
that never fell, staying encased in
          memories of warmer days.

Snowfall

One of my mother's last wishes
was to smell winter
       after a late March snowfall.
It was always special as a child
to be the one
whose turn it was to walk with her
the evening of the
       first storm of the season,
making new footprints around
the snow-muffled neighborhood
as streetlights came on,
creating magical misty halos.
She said snowflakes
were angel kisses as we lifted our
       faces towards the sky.

Backside of The Night Stars

I looked up into the sky
the night my mother died,
and felt the void
of her earthly presence.

When my daughter died,
I had a star in some distant galaxy
named for her,
to burn forever in my heart.

The night before my father died,
I did a salutation to the January moon
in a clear space outside my home,
feeling the pull
of cold white light.

My husband loved the first sliver
of the quarter moon,
bright in the vivid blue of twilight –
the time of day he slipped
into a downward spiral until he
was gone.

When the night is
bright with constellations,
I think of those I love
scattered across the country,
the world,
        on the backside of the night stars,
knowing somehow they are
seeing the same sky.

Tracing Orion,
        we are connected.

Our Time
   (for Chloé)

You were the flame
that kept me going,
the light of hope
after my mother died,
kindling in my womb.

Just four months after
she took her last breath,
you never took your first.

Ripped from me,
red blood seeped into
a tiny white coffin.

A piece of me died that day,
a faint white scar
traces the space where you
once were.

Light
  (for my son, Luc)

Your name means light.
As on that brilliant autumn morning
you first opened your eyes
            to the world and smiled,
you have embraced your life
by always following
the beat of your own rhythms.
You taught me how to just be
              in the moment
as I watched you grow.

You bring back the light
for me,
the music in my soul.

Frozen Tears

I walk the streets of the city
during another festive season
                    without you.
Tears sting my eyes from the bitter cold,
yet I embrace them,
                    let them fall freely,
masquerading the
tears of warmer times,
that flow from the depths
of so many memories
that slowly extinguished
                    our flame.

"Public Gardens, Boston"

Winter Kiss

The morning forest sparkles
with freshly fallen snow.
The air is pure, clean.

I recall our first winter kiss
                          in the park
in the heart of the city
where we met during an autumn sunset.

The warmth melting frozen lips.

You, who loved summertime,
became enchanted in the silence
              of the muffled softness.

We were the only two people
                      in that space,
enveloped in newly found love.

Sliding

I walk city streets,
barren of ice for now.
The misshapen bricks
                    taunt me,
knowing they can glaze over,
sending a confident walker
into an indefinite slide,
much like life,
unknowing when
            an innocent step
leads to an unfortunate future.

Prisms

Spectral colors
shimmer on the
     black granite countertop
late afternoons,
during this vigil
I've been keeping,
marking the weeks,
the days, and soon,
     the hours until you left,
two years ago on the
twenty-second day of the second month.
White light,
     pure as the relentless snow that winter,
disperses into tiny rainbows,
catching me on some
otherworldly wavelength.

"Snow-laced Beach"

Seeds

Sadness is a seed
that sits in your soul.
Tears make it swell
    at unexpected times.
A thought, a memory
can bring on a river of salty rain
    crashing down your cheeks
pooling in a broken heart.

Joy is a seed
that sits in your soul.
An unexpected encounter,
a snow-laced sunset
    on a late winter beach,
a memory of warmer days,
of knowing love,
filling your mending heart.

"Together — Apart"

Swan Song

Our paths first crossed at sunset
in a Boston park where swans
performed their evening pas de deux ,
        pure white feathers turning pale amber.

Sacred to Venus in Roman mythology,
swans exude beauty and grace – and love.
        Tête-à-tête, a pair forms the shape
            of a heart.

We watched the day fade into twilight.
You told me I had sad eyes.
You did not know then,
they were mirrors
        of survival.

The swan became our totem,
symbolizing transformation,
as we navigated a new life together.

In some cultures swans are linked to angels,
divine healing,
and mystical journeys
        to the otherworld.

I circle life's pond alone,
a solo swan song
        plays over and over.

CPSIA information can be obtained at www.ICGtesting.com
Printed in the USA
BVIW12n0923091017
496675BV00001B/1

* 9 7 8 1 9 4 4 3 9 3 6 0 1 *